ELDERS & FYFFES

A PHOTOGRAPHIC HISTORY

The *Bayano* (II) and *Carare* at Avonmouth in 1928, the year *Bayano* opened the new dock extension at Avonmouth.

ELDERS & FYFFES

A PHOTOGRAPHIC HISTORY

CAMPBELL MCCUTCHEON

AMBERLEY

Changuinola (II) at Southampton on 31 August 1968.

First published 2010
This edition published 2016

Amberley Publishing
The Hill, Stroud
Gloucestershire, GL5 4EP
www.amberley-books.com

Copyright © Campbell McCutcheon, 2015

The right of Campbell McCutcheon to be identified as the Author of this work has been asserted in accordance with the Copyrights, Designs and Patents Act 1988.

ISBN 978 1 4456 5621 2 (print)
ISBN 978 1 4456 2339 9 (print)

British Library Cataloguing in Publication Data.

A catalogue record for this book is available from the British Library.

Typeset in 10pt on 12pt Celeste OT.
Typesetting and Origination by Amberley Publishing.
Printed in the UK.

CONTENTS

Golfito at sea, *c.* 1950.

INTRODUCTION

Bananas! They're a simple fruit; versatile, expertly packaged and tasty too. However, the banana was once an unknown commodity in the UK as it was difficult to transport the thousands of miles from where it was grown to markets in the UK. Early attempts to bring the golden fruit to the UK saw ships full of boxes of black, overripe bananas which had turned to mush and had to be shoveled out of their holds. The sailing ship was simply too slow and suffered from the heat of the tropics when the bananas were exported. Even carriage on the faster steamships caused the bananas to go bad. Only when methods of transportation had been worked out by trial and error did it become viable to attempt to import bananas to northern Europe. For many places, such as the Canary Islands, bananas had long been a subsistence foodstuff, grown for local consumption but with little thought for the export market. So how did the humble banana become a staple of our diet here in the UK?

Strangely, the story starts not a million miles from where this book is published. Edward Wathan Fyffe (yes, the Fyffe of Fyffes bananas) was born at Woodchester, near Stroud, about four miles from the offices of the publisher of this book. He owned a house in Box, near Minchinhampton, and died in 1935. Buried in the churchyard at Amberley (yes, the village, the publisher is named after), how did he become synonymous with the banana and who was Mr Elder? The story of the banana in Britain and Europe and Elders & Fyffes is intertwined and within the following pages, I will hopefully tell the story of how and why the line was set up, its ultimate purchase by the Americans and the history of the men and ships of Elders & Fyffes. Like many partnerships, the story of Elders & Fyffes is a story of two halves, each bringing a different expertise to the company. Elder Dempster had the shipping and banana importation experience while Fyffe's could sell fruit. It was a match made in banana heaven.

The banana does encourage some fun though and it would be remiss of me not to include within the pages of this short book some banana facts, some useful to know and some totally useless. For example, the banana is the world's largest non-woody plant, and is also the world's largest herb. It is related to the plantain. As far as is known, it was first imported in quantity into Britain in 1884 by none other than Elder Dempster's.

The catalyst for its importation was the use of the Canary Islands as a water and coal bunkering stop for ships from the west coast of Africa. One of the major lines operating in the area was Elder Dempster and its African Steamship Co. After some trial and error, it started importing bananas as deck cargo on its ships. The imported bananas found a ready market and became popular around Liverpool. Their ripe state when they arrived precluded any wider distribution and, by the end of the decade, merchants began to look at ways of getting bananas to the UK and ensuring they still had some shelf life when they got here. Elder Dempster's had set up a fruit brokerage in London to go with the company's other non-shipping activities and were experienced in transporting the delicate fruits long distances without them over-ripening.

Edward Wathan Fyffe was the chairman of E. W. Fyffe & Co., a tea importer of some note. It was a chance visit to the Canary Islands, where Cavendish bananas (*Musaceae Cavendishii*) were grown, with his wife Ida, who was recuperating from tuberculosis, that led Fyffe to look at the possibilities of importing bananas into Great Britain. By 1888, Fyffe's was importing large quantities of Cavendish bananas to London, selling them wholesale. A banana then was 2*d*, which is about £1 at today's prices, so was more of a luxury item than a staple food. Packed green, into wooden boxes, the bananas would reach London, hopefully, just as they started to ripen, giving about five days to sell them before they went off. Any delay had a huge impact on the quality of the fruit and hence its price. Fyffe realised, though, that there was a huge potential for the banana and he started to shift his company's trading base away from tea to the more lucrative banana. The senior partner of Elder Dempster, Alfred Lewis Jones, had seen the huge profits from importing bananas into Liverpool and he too encouraged the growth of the business in London. These two men, Fyffe and Jones, can claim to be the first banana entrepreneurs in Britain.

Fyffe's was a wholesale company and they sold most of their stock directly to Hudson Bros, a major fruit seller in London, and by 1896, it made sense for the two companies to merge, which they did in 1897, to become Fyffe, Hudson & Co. The biggest result of this was that Edward Fyffe sold his share of Fyffe's when the new company was formed and he retired to the Stroud valleys, aged forty-four. Despite the new company having the name 'Fyffe', no Fyffes were involved in it anymore.

Meanwhile, Elder Dempster was approached by the Colonial Secretary, Jospeh Chamberlain, and was asked whether it would form a company to import the larger Jamaican banana (*Musaceae sapientum*) from the West Indies. Alfred Jones sent out his Fruit Department manager, one Arthur H. Stockley, to Jamaica. Trials showed that the fruit would ripen during the almost two-week journey and arrive in Britain unusable.

After a failed attempt at setting up the Jamaica Produce Co. in 1899, to make twenty-six sailings a year, each bringing at least 20,000 arms of bananas to Britain, Chamberlain tried again the following year. This time, the lure of a £30,000 per annum mail contract saw the setting up of the Imperial Direct West India Mail Service by Elder Dempster. The new line was to be based in Avonmouth, and would only serve Jamaica. And it is here that the story of Elders & Fyffes begins properly. Of course, the answer to 'Who was Mr Elder?', is that Mr Elder had no connection with Elders & Fyffes whatsoever! He had long retired from the shipping company which bore his name.

In the mid-1970s, Elders & Fyffes chartered ships, rather than purchased them and I have deliberately taken the history up to the 1970s, and excluded the more recent vessels, which have not directly been owned by the company. The ships of Geest, a company that Elders & Fyffes amalgamated with in 1986, are also not included. Within the pages, though, I have tried to include an image of almost every vessel owned by the company, including a couple of inter-island tenders. The ships of Fyffes were no stranger to accident either and I have included, where possible views of ships that have been sunk, run aground or that have otherwise 'gone bump in the night.' The visual feast within these pages also includes launchings, final voyages and scrappings, as well as ships in liveries of former or new owners. I sincerely hope you enjoy the following and apologise for any errors or omissions within.

Little of note has been written on Fyffes but the company has had a few superb books written about it. Sources for this book include the following books, for which I am grateful.

Merchant Fleets 31 Elders & Fyffes
Yes We have Bananas
Fyffes & the Banana
The White Ship

One has to thank the many photographers who took the images I have used. Some, like B. A. Fielden, of Liverpool, W. Robertson, of Gourock, the Nautical Photo Agency, and Garrett, of Bristol, I know, but many are unidentified and therefore, unknown. To all the unknown photographers, and those I know, many thanks for taking such an interesting selection of images of the banana boats of Elders & Fyffes. Without them, this book would have never been possible. All images are from my collection and I was lucky enough to buy, about seven years ago, a large collection of Fyffes photos that had once belonged to a Captain Hugh Chubb, who commanded more than one Fyffes banana boat, and this has been supplemented by postcards and photos from my own collection. The choice of what to use and what to leave out is always difficult, and the following represents the whittling down of many hundreds of images into the 220 or so you see here. I have tried to use the best images, over a variety of locations from Garston, Liverpool and Preston to Southampton, Newhaven, Cardiff and Avonmouth, as well as Jamaica, Columbia, Rotterdam, Bruges and Bremen. Enjoy the book and 'Have a Banana!'

A banana walk, Kingston, Jamaica.

The SS *Golden Eagle*, of 213 tons, was built in 1877 and acquired by Elders &
Fyffes as an inter-island coaster. She was renamed *Aguila del Oro*, as shown here,
probably at Las Palmas.

Fyffes needed distribution networks in the UK to grow and expand. This view shows a banana cart displayed at a gala day or fair, most likely in Lancashire, *c.* 1910.

Above left: The passenger service to the West Indies was important and Elders & Fyffes issued advertising postcards extolling the virtues of cruises to Jamaica.

Above right: The Elders & Fyffes logo.

Left: A 1920s comic postcard with a banana theme. Fyffes cleverly engineered some of this publicity themselves, but sometimes it was generated for them by the use of bananas in songs such as *Let's All Go Down the Strand*.

Chapter One

GOING BANANAS – ELDER DEMPSTER, IMPERIAL DIRECT & THE FYFFES CONNECTION

Going Bananas – an idiom that dates back to at least 1935, and made popular in the late 1960s when it was believed by students that roasted banana skins had psychedelic properties similar to 'magic mushrooms' and that the effects made you high, or crazy.

In 1900, Joseph Chamberlain finally succeeded in encouraging Elder Dempster's to set up a subsidiary to import bananas from Jamaica. With a £40,000 initial subsidy and a £30,000 per annum mail subsidy, the new line, the Imperial Direct West India Mail Service was set up. With Jamaica paying half the cost per year, Imperial Direct only had to find an outward cargo. With the failure of Jamaica Produce Co. its ships became available. They were still building and it was possible for Imperial Direct to have them lengthened by 30 ft to accommodate both refrigeration plant and the 100 First Class and 50 worker berths stipulated in the contract with the government. Alfred Jones owned 18,000 of the initial 25,000 shares in the company. These two ships became *Port Morant* and *Port Maria*. Despite their lengthening on the stocks, they both proved to be too small and two new ships were ordered to supplement them.

These two new vessels, *Port Royal* and *Port Antonio*, were both built at Middlesbrough and were a good 40 ft longer than their earlier sisters. *Port Henderson* was then transferred from Elder Dempster's Beaver Line subsidiary in 1905. The last new ship built for the fleet came in 1904; *Port Kingston* was the largest ship on the route till Elders & Fyffes *Golfito* was built in 1949.

Of course, having simply auctioned off the stock of bananas previously, Elder Dempster, via Imperial Direct, now owned 40,000 stems of bananas a month. Arthur Stockley had become general manager of Imperial Direct and he discussed plans with Alfred Jones. To guarantee a crop to ensure the ships were profitable, would mean that the line would have to invest in plantations, as well as warehousing and specialist handling equipment in the UK and a distribution service to rapidly transport bananas to every part of the land. It was too big a job for Elder Dempster and would require a separate company with the experience of plantations, shipping, storage, distribution and sales. The quantity of fruit imported each month made the investment worthwhile too.

The first ships built for Imperial Direct were *Port Morant* and *Port Maria*. Shown here is *Port Morant* on her maiden arrival into Avonmouth. She was built by Alexander Stephen of Linthouse, Glasgow, for Captain Lamont but purchased by Elder Dempster while under construction. She was lengthened by 30 ft and inaugurated the Avonmouth–Kingston service on 16 February 1901. She landed 18,000 stems of bananas back in Avonmouth on 18 March 1901. In 1904, she was replaced by *Port Kingston* and laid up. In 1905, she transferred to the Elder Line Ltd and was sold to Argentina in 1909. In the same month as the *Titanic* sank, she too was lost, wrecked in the Straits of Magellan. *Port Maria* was built by Ramage & Ferguson, Leith, but was essentially identical to *Port Morant*. She lasted through various owners until 1933 and was broken up at La Spezia.

Above and right: Two advert postcards for the Imperial Direct Line. Despite being a financial failure, passenger traffic to Jamaica was good and the company issued many postcards extolling the virtue of Jamaica.

IMPERIAL DIRECT WEST INDIA MAIL SERVICE Co Ld.

MENU

BREAKFAST   20·9·05

Oranges   Bananas   Avocado Pears

Quaker Oats   Grape Nuts

Smoked Haddock

Salmon Croquettes

Minced Collops

Macaroni Milanaise

Rognons Saute aux Champignons

Chops and Steak (to order 10 minutes)

Eggs (to order anyway required)

Grilled Bacon on Toast

Chip, Shred and Mashed Potatoes

Curry and Rice

COLD

Cumberland Ham   Ox Tongue   Roast Beef

Semolina Cakes

Toast   Hot Rolls   Vienna and Brown Bread

Guava Jelly   Jam   Honey   Marmalade

Tea   Coffee   Cocoa

Chocolate

Left: Passengers were well catered for. This is a typical breakfast menu from 20 September 1905, probably from *Port Henderson*.

Below: The sisters *Port Royal* and *Port Antonio* were built at Dixon's yard in Middlesbrough. Both were of 370 ft in length and of 4,455 grt. Each lasted until the end of the line in 1911. *Port Royal* was sold to Turkey and was lost in 1914 when sunk by a Russian warship in November.

ROARING RIVER FALLS, JAMAICA

R.M.S. PORT ROYAL

MYRTLE BANK HOTEL, JAMAICA.

Above and right: Port Antonio and her sister were the classic design of banana boat and it would remain almost unchanged for thirty years. Sold to Turkey in 1911 and used as a hospital ship in the war, she became part of the Turkish navy in 1933.

CONSTANT SPRING HOTEL, JAMAICA

R.M.S. PORT HENDERSON

IMPERIAL DIRECT WEST INDIA MAIL SERVICE CO.y LTD

Left: Launched in 1884, *Port Henderson* had originally been Shaw, Savill & Albion's *Arawa*. She led a chequered career for numerous shipping lines, but came into Imperial Direct service in 1905 and replaced *Port Morant*, which was simply too small for the service. She was the only secondhand tonnage bought by the line.

Right: Port Kingston was built by Alexander Stephen in 1904 and could carry 160 First Class and 60 Second Class passengers. She was the largest ship on the route until 1949. Sold in 1911 to the Union Steamship Co. of New Zealand, she became *Tahiti*. She sank on 17 August 1930 after her propeller shaft broke and punctured her hull on the fifteenth. In two days she had gone, but the passengers, crew, their luggage and gold bullion aboard were all saved.

IMPERIAL DIRECT WEST INDIA MAIL SERVICE CO.y LTD

R.M.S. PORT KINGSTON

Peep at the RIO COBRE...JAMAICA

Chapter Two

HAVE A BANANA – ELDERS & FYFFES IS FOUNDED

'Have a Banana' comes from the popular music hall song, *Let's All Go Down the Strand*

The separate organisation that Stockley had in mind was an entirely new company, bringing together the experience of the different parts of the new business. He had secret talks with Fyffe, Hudson & Co., who saw the immense potential that this new business could have. They would bring their wholesale and retail skills to the table, while Elder Dempster would bring the ship operating skills, as well as the vessels required. Stockley introduced the idea to Alfred Jones, who quickly assumed that Stockley and Fyffe, Hudson could start such a business themselves. Ever the businessman, Jones agreed to help fund the business. With Imperial Direct still loss-making, he was reluctant at first, but in May 1901, Elders & Fyffes was born. With a share capital of £150,000, the sum of £60,000 was raised to start the business. Jones owned just under half the shares, while his friend William Davey owned a controlling balance, effectively giving Jones overall control and the chairmanship. Arthur Stockley became managing director, and the three Fyffe, Hudson directors became directors too. A small share was owned by the Bristol towage company, C. J. King, and the home port would be Avonmouth.

With almost a decade to run, the Imperial Direct contract with the government could not be broken and it was decided to operate the new service in conjunction with Imperial Direct, thereby giving a weekly service, which was required to feed the distribution and sales facilities. As a consequence, three suitable secondhand cattle carriers were bought from Furness, Withy in 1902 and converted with refrigeration equipment for their new trade. In that year, almost £50,000 of bananas, represented by 643,846 stems, had been imported. However, despite this success, about 50 per cent of the crop landed was damaged, while hurricanes had wreaked havoc in some plantations. The company was in trouble and Jones was reluctant to use any more of his cash to bale it out. Arthur Stockley travelled to Boston to meet with the United Fruit Company, which had huge plantations in the Indies and Central America. He hoped to broker a deal whereby the UFC would sell Elders & Fyffes surplus bananas if Fyffes could not load enough from their own plantations.

The deal came with conditions, one of which was that United Fruit wanted to buy into the company. This suited Jones, who wanted to reduce his shareholding anyway. As the line had to remain British, United Fruit purchased 45 per cent of Elders & Fyffes and agreed to guarantee cargoes. A new ship was bought, and it opened a new Manchester service, serving northern England. In 1903, hurricanes devastated the Jamaican crop and the Fyffes and Imperial Direct ships loaded in Costa Rica instead, saving Fyffes from going bust, as they would have done if they had had to rely on Jamaican bananas alone.

By 1904, fortunes had turned and Elders & Fyffes began to order their first brand-new ships, with *Matina* being the first. A year later, the first Fyffes bananas were sold in Norway and the Netherlands. In 1906, Charles McCann became the Irish distributor. In a roundabout way, Charles McCann's company now owns the Fyffes brand. Three years later, Alfred Jones died, aged sixty-four. His executors sold the various Elder Dempster companies in one lump to Royal Mail Group and Harland & Wolff. Elders & Fyffes remained separate and it was expected that its directors would buy the company but it was sold instead to United Fruit. Despite the disappointment, the company was left untouched and ran as before.

The new owners of Imperial Direct took the opportunity in 1911 to close down the loss-making subsidiary (the only one of Elder Dempster's companies which reported a loss). Despite making a loss on the freight side, Imperial Direct's ships had always travelled full. With ten ships, Fyffes could carry on a weekly service without the Imperial Direct vessels, but they viewed the passenger trade with interest and the next series of vessels could all accommodate fifty passengers. On 1 January 1912, the Manchester berth was closed and a new depot opened at Garston's Stalbridge Dock.

Left: In 1902, Elders & Fyffes purchased their first ships. All four vessels were secondhand and constructed by Furness, Withy in West Hartlepool for the Chesapeake & Ohio Steamship Co., running from Newport News, VA, to the UK. The first of the new fleet was *Appomattox*, with *Chickahominy*, *Greenbrier* and *Oracabessa* making the quartet. *Appomattox* was named after one of the last battles of the American Civil War. This view shows her in her C&O colours. She was used as a cattle carrier, capable of carrying 500 cattle and general cargo.

Above left: The date is July 1903 and *Appomattox* is unloading at Salford, having traversed the Manchester Ship Canal. When purchased by E&F, she, like her sisters, was converted with refrigeration plant, her holds wood-lined and partitioned, and was capable of carrying 25,000 bunches of bananas on a fourteen-day journey from the West Indies to England, with a maximum speed of 11.5 kt.

Above right: Rust-stained, *Appomottax* in the Mersey, *c.* 1910. In this year, she and her sisters were sold. In *Appomottax*'s case, to Turkey, where she was renamed *Seyer*. She became a war loss in 1916, having been sunk by the Russian destroyer *Zongduldak*.

Right: Chickahominy was named after a tribe of Virginia Native Americans. She had a tonnage of 3,354 grt and made the first call by a Fyffes ship at Salford, carrying 50,000 stems there in 1902. 400 stevedores unloaded the cargo in an amazing twelve hours. Sold in 1910, she was broken for scrap in Garston after a career of seventeen years. Here, she is seen in the Bristol Channel in 1905 on a rare, but damaged, postcard.

Left: Chickahominy berthed, *c.* 1908. This view shows her figurehead rather well. The portholes along the main deck were there as the ships were designed as cattle carriers originally, hence their higher than average top speeds. The four ships were fitted with triple-expansion engines powered by two double boilers powering a single screw, as was typical of general cargo vessels of the time.

Right: Christmas 1902 saw *Greenbrier* loading bananas in Jamaica. On 25 December, as her engines were started to leave, she lost her single propeller, a rather scary, but none too infrequent occurrence. Only the refrigeration equipment saved the cargo while a new propeller was fitted. *Greenbrier* was named after an area of Virginia, which houses a famous hotel that once belonged to the Chesapeake & Ohio Railway. This view shows *Greenbrier* in the Mersey. She was sold to the Tropical Fruit & Shipping Co., owned by United Fruit Co. On 2 April 1915, she was transferred to the American flag but sunk by a mine off the Frisian Islands en route from Bremerhaven to New York.

Left: The last of the original four ships was *Oracabessa*, built in 1894 by Wm Doxford, Sunderland. She saw a name change from her original *Carlisle City*. Built for Furness, Withy, she was replaced in 1902 and sold to Fyffes in 1903 for use on the Manchester route. A common cargo on the return route was South Wales steam coal. While taking a cargo of coal from Barry to Port Limon, she rescued the crew of the sailing vessel *Cambrian Hills* on 8 March 1905.

Right: The name *Oracabessa* (Spanish for 'Golden Head') comes from a Jamaican town which lost its banana wharves in 1969. In 1909, *Oracabessa* was sold. Her name was changed in 1916, when she became the Brazilian *Belem*. She had the longest career of the first four ships, being scrapped in 1932 at Rio de Janeiro.

Above: In 1904, the banana business was so busy and so profitable that E&F expanded, building three new ships: *Matina, Miami* and *Manistee.* The first of the trio, *Manistee,* was built by Swan, Hunter & Wigham Richardson on the Tyne and completed in March 1904. Refrigeration was by air-cooling over cold brine pipes. This view shows *Matina* at Salford.

Right: *Mariposa* (I) was originally used as a tender in the Canary Islands but was moved to Jamaica in 1924.

Left: Matina in the Mersey, rapidly overhauling a sailing vessel. She was one of the last ships to be broken at Morecambe, on the site of what is now the Midland Hotel.

Below: Miami was built in Glasgow, at Barclay, Curle & Co., and had a registered tonnage of 3,762. All three ships had four single boilers powering triple expansion steam engines. *Miami* at Manchester, *c.* 1910.

Left: On 22 June 1917, in the Western Approaches, off Fastnet Rock, *Miami* was sunk by *UC-51*. She was en route from New York to Manchester with a general cargo.

Right: Completed a month after her sisters, *Manistee* was sunk four days after *Miami*, 86 miles from the Scillies by the German submarine *U-62*. Five crew died on what should have been a run from New York to London with general cargo. Also built by Swan, Hunter on the Tyne, she is shown here in Manchester.

Above left: *Manistee*, when new, in Manchester.

Above right: A rather battered postcard view showing the stern of *Manistee* (I), and posted from Liverpool on 3 November 1909. The message reads, 'this ship is full up with passengers'.

Right: Between 1905 and 1909, a further seven ships were added to the E&F fleet. The first, of 3,911 grt, was built by Alexander Stephen, Linthouse, and named *Nicoya*. In August 1914, she was detained by the Germans when delivering a cargo of bananas in Hamburg and used as a store ship for the duration of the war. As a result she survived the First World War. She is shown here, post-war, berthed in the Mersey.

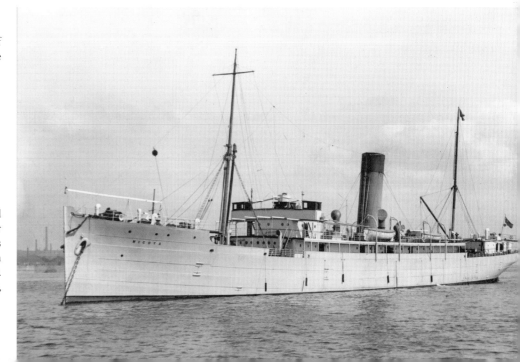

Above: Pacuare was the first E&F ship built in Ireland, at Workman, Clark's Belfast yard. In 1913, she made the first regular calls into Amsterdam and survived a U-boat attack on 18 August 1916. Shown here outward bound from a West Indian port before the war.

Below: Zent was completed in April 1906. She is shown here at Avonmouth *c.* 1910. Lost off Fastnet on 5 April 1916 bound from Garston to Santa Marta, Columbia, with the loss of her entire crew of forty-nine.

1906.

Above left and right: Barranca was registered in Manchester and was based there. The first view of her, from a period postcard, shows her in Salford in April 1906 before her maiden voyage from the port. Interestingly, she was torpedoed during the First World War while operating as the Q-ship *Echunga.* She survived the attack on 26 April 1917 and was towed to Portsmouth for repair.

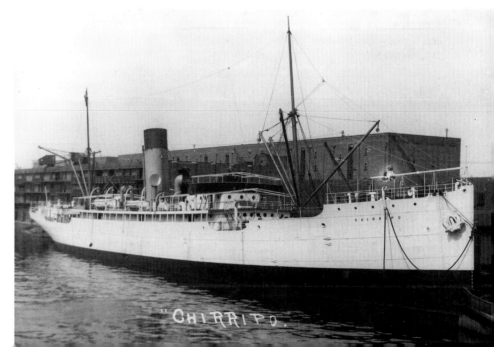

Right: Chirripo at Manchester, *c.* 1910. Also built at Workman, Clark and completed in May 1906, *Chirripo* spent her war on commercial service but was mined off Black Head.

Left: Chirripo flying her 'Blue Peter' and ready to sail from Avonmouth to the West Indies, *c.* 1912.

Right: Completed at Workman, Clark a bare month after *Chirripo, Reventazon* was lost near Salonika while en route to Port Said on 5 October 1918. She was a victim of a torpedo from *UC-23*.

Left: The last of the seven vessels was *Tortuguero*, built in 1909. Her engine power was reduced as it was considered that the engines of her six sisters were too powerful for the service requirement. She is shown here, probably at Santa Marta, Columbia.

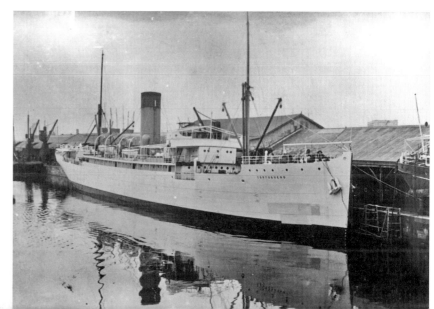

Right: Tortuguero, bound for Jamaica on 26 June 1918, was sunk by *U-156*, with the loss of twelve crew.

Left: In 1911 came two improved *Nicoya*-class vessels; one from Workman, Clark, the other from Alexander Stephen. *Aracataca*, shown here, was the Irish vessel. With a slight increase in size to 4,154 grt, and the reduced-power engines, she could carry twelve passengers. On 10 March 1917, she was attacked by a submarine but escaped with a speed of 15.5 kt, which just shows that the reduced power did little to affect top speed. A month and a week after surviving the attack by *U-44*, she collided with the Lamport & Holt vessel *Moliere* and sank off Beachy Head.

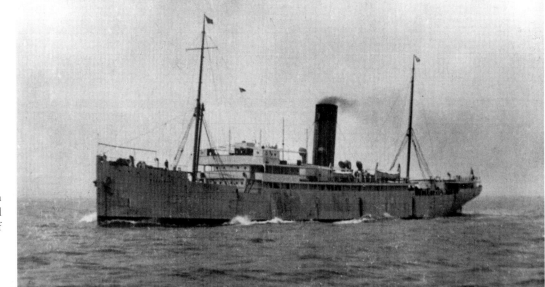

Right: The Glasgow-built *Manzanares* remained in commercial service throughout the war and was sold in 1935. Renamed *Vegesack*, she was wrecked off Stavanger, Norway, a mere four years later, in 1939.

Left: In 1912 came a series of four passenger ships, capable of carrying about fifty passengers each, in comparison to the twelve of the previous Fyffes vessels. Two each came from the company's preferred builders of the time, Workman, Clark and Alexander Stephen of Linthouse. Each could carry 150,000 stems of bananas, about triple the quantity of the older vessels. *Chagres* was the first of the new ships and she is shown here. She lasted a mere six years before being sunk by submarine.

Below: Second of the class was the first *Patia*, built at Belfast. She was of 6,103 grt.

Left: Patia at Garston, *c.* 1913.

Right: The first *Bayano* on her sea trials off Scotland, 1913. Converted to an armed merchant cruiser at Avonmouth, she was torpedoed by *U-27* and sank within four minutes off Corsewall Point, Wigtownshire, on 11 March 1917. There were twenty-six survivors and 197 casualties.

Left: A stern view of *Bayano* (I) at Avonmouth 1914. This class was the first to have twin screws.

Right: *Patuca* at Avonmouth and the only ship of the class to survive the war. She was based at Scapa Flow as part of the 10th Cruiser Squadron. Broken up in the Netherlands in 1935.

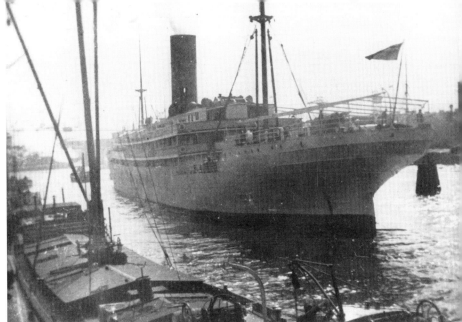

Above: A stern view of *Patuca*.

Left: Originally destined for the Hamburg Amerika Line's Atlas subsidiary, the *Changuinola* and *Motagua* were both built by Swan, Hunter & Wigham Richardson on the Tyne in 1912. After being acquired by United Fruit Co., they were transferred to Fyffes in 1914. *Changuinola*, shown here in dry dock, survived until 1933 before being broken on the Clyde.

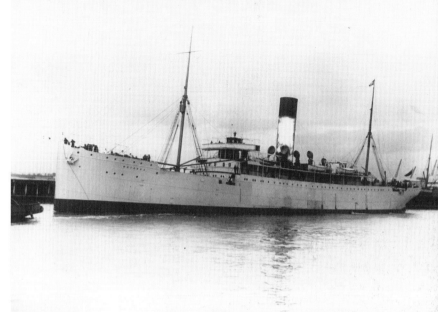

Above left: Changuinola at Avonmouth.

Above right: Motagua at Avonmouth in 1914, with the Canadian Northern Line's Royal Edward or Royal George astern of her. Royal Edward was sunk during the First World War with the loss of over 1,000 lives, while her sister survived to become a Cunard ship, nicknamed the 'Rolling George' as she was a top-heavy design.

Right: Loading bananas at Santa Marta, Columbia. Santa Marta has been much built up since this view was taken in c. 1914.

Chapter Three

TOP BANANA – THE FIRST WORLD WAR

Top Banana – the starring act in a Vaudeville show. The phrase was first used by Harry Steppe, a famous Vaudeville performer.

In March 1914, two ships were added to the fleet via a complicated deal with Hamburg Amerika Line. Both were passenger-carrying vessels. Five months later, the 'war to end all wars' started and many of the fleet were called up for service. Entering the war with sixteen vessels, despite adding some during the war, Elders & Fyffes finished it with eleven. Ten ships were lost, including *Patia* and the almost brand new *Bayano*, which saw less than eighteen months of service for Elders & Fyffes and His Majesty.

Left: Two crew members of *Manzaneres* look down onto Garratt, the local Bristol postcard publisher, as he photographs their vessel. Next to her is the first *Camito*. This vessel was constructed in 1915 by Alexander Stephen and launched on 15 April that year. She survived the war, but not after being attacked by a submarine and hitting a mine. She was not so lucky in the Second World War and was lost to *U-97*, while escorting an Italian tanker, which had been captured by the Allies.

Right: Garratt has wandered round the end of the dock, showing the sterns of both *Camito* and *Manzaneres*.

A rare view of *Camito*'s sister, *Cavina*. She entered service in 1915 but was sunk a mere two years later, on 1 June 1917, while en route from Santa Marta, Columbia, to Avonmouth with a cargo of bananas and timber. Both ships were of 6,600 grt. The third sister, *Coronado*, was also built at Workman, Clark's but survived the war to be broken in Italy.

The only Bristol survivor of the sinking of *Bayano* (I) off Scotland, Mr Abner Witcombe, of 40 Redfield Road, Bristol, is shown wearing the 'bib'. Only twenty-six survived the sinking.

Coronado was launched on April Fool's Day, 1915 and immediately converted to an ocean boarding vessel, to stop and search neutral ships for contraband destined for Germany and her allies. In 1917, she was attacked by *U-24* but chased her off with her gunfire and was then torpedoed by U 55 and towed into Queenstown. Repaired, she entered service for Elders & Fyffes in March 1919, reopening their Avonmouth passenger service. In 1935, she was broken for scrap at La Spezia, Italy. Her dazzle-paint scheme is shown to good effect in this view of her, *c.* 1917.

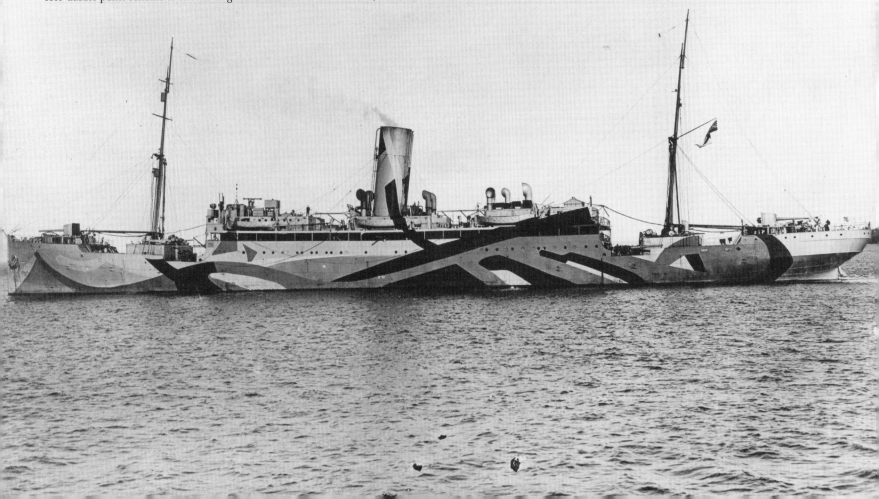

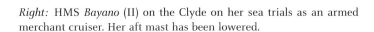

Above left and right: Ordered as *Cauca*, but launched as *Bayano* (II) to replace the ship of the same name lost that year, this vessel had hinged masts and a straight funnel designed to confuse U-boats.

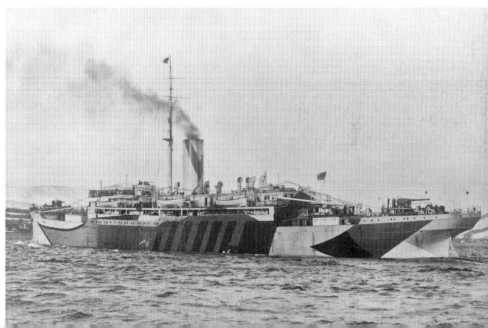

Right: HMS *Bayano* (II) on the Clyde on her sea trials as an armed merchant cruiser. Her aft mast has been lowered.

Above and below: HMS *Patia* as an armed merchant cruiser in 1917/18. Her service took her from Senegal to north of Iceland. These snapshots show her armaments, which composed of six 6-in guns. While suited to the balmy waters off Senegal, the ship was not designed for the North Atlantic and the chilly seas off Iceland.

Opposite: Views from the crow's nest of HMS *Patia* in Loch Ewe, 10 July 1917.

Above: The visible additions to the superstructure, as well as the bow gun, can clearly be seen on this view of *Patia* in 1917.

Right: A waterlogged lifeboat is brought aboard HMS *Patia* on 3 June 1917.

Left: An unknown Fyffes AMC in Dakar, Senegal, most likely HMS *Patuga*. Dazzle-painting was a unique camouflage developed by Norman Wilkinson, the famous marine artist, as a way of disguising a ship. The disruptive paintwork was designed to confuse a submarine captain as to the speed and direction of travel of his intended victim.

Right: On 13 June 1918, in the Bristol Channel, HMS *Patia* was torpedoed by *UC-69* and sank.

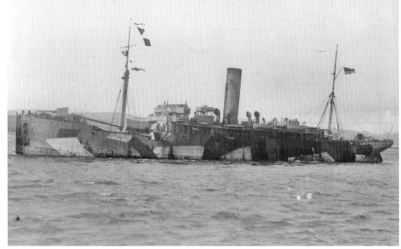

Above left: HMS *Patuca* was the fifth Fyffes ship to serve with the Navy and the only ship of her class to survive the war. Here she is as part of the 10th Cruiser Sqaudron.

Above right: Changuinola flying her White Ensign while dazzle-painted.

Left: The 6-in gun on the poop deck of HMS *Changuinola*.

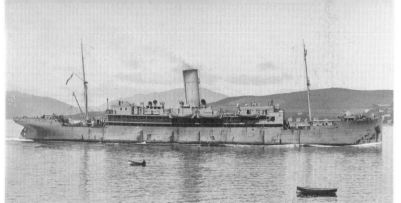

Above: HMS *Aracataca* photographed on the Clyde by Wm Robertson, perhaps one of the best maritime photographers of all time. Robertson took many photos from the Pilot Station at Greenock and at one time had a shop selling his photos in Royal Exchange Square, Glasgow.

Left: On 16 March 1917, *Motagua* struck a mine off the Shetlands but safely made port and was repaired. The following year, in March 1918, she collided with the US destroyer USS *Manley*. Her stern was blown off by depth charges from the *Manley*. Miraculously, she made port yet again and was repaired, surviving until 1933, then was broken up at Rotterdam.

Below: Another view of *Motagua* in her war colours, painted battleship grey.

Chapter Four

UP THE CLYDE IN A BANANA BOAT – THE INTERWAR YEARS

Do You Think I Came Up the Clyde in a Banana Boat? – a Glaswegian expression which translates to 'Do You Think I'm Stupid?' The Aberdonian equivalent is '... Doon the Dee oan a Digestive?'

The end of the war saw new ships added to replace the ships lost, including a famous ex-German commerce raider, the *Moewe*, which became *Greenbrier*. In 1920 came the first of nineteen standard ships, built by Cammell Laird and Alexander Stephen. The global expansion of Elders & Fyffes began as they expanded the fleet, with new companies formed in France (1922), the Netherlands (1925) and Germany (1926). In May 1926, at the start of the General Strike, with five fully-laden ships in port, all available Elders & Fyffes staff descended on Avonmouth and Garston and emptied the vessels of 100,000 stems of bananas, with all the fruit being transshipped by road.

A new connection with the Canaries was made in 1927, with the building of three smaller ships for the route, while, by 1930, 193,400 tons of bananas were being imported into Britain on thirty-six vessels. Little thought was given to outward cargo and all efforts made to speed the turnaround of the ships so they could make as many voyages as possible. Despite taking a year to grow, bananas will grow at any time of year and so are easily harvestable at any time.

United Fruit expanded in 1931, with the addition of the Cuyamel Fruit Co., and transferred three of their vessels to Elders & Fyffes. In 1933, with the Nazis in power in Germany, it was almost impossible to get currency out of the country, and so a fully German subsidiary, 'Union' Handels-und-Schiffahrtsgesellschaft GmbH, was formed, and four ships transferred. Some clever deals in 1936, with Jamaica Banana Producers S.S. Co. saw United Fruit remove its North American competition and give Elders & Fyffes only three foreign ships to worry about. The companies effectively monopolised the trade. The following year saw the liquidation of the Canary Islands subsidiary due to the Spanish Civil War.

Above left: Greenbrier (II) was a war prize and formerly the German auxiliary cruiser *Moewe*. In December 1915, she left on the hunt for Allied victims and sank fifteen vessels. Her second cruise saw her destroy only a single ship, while her third saw twenty-one vessels at the bottom of the sea. Ceded to Britain as war reparation, she ended up with Elders & Fyffes in 1921. Conversion work involved creating holds over four decks to hold bananas and creating a ventilation system that saw cold air pumped down one side of the ship and warm air sucked out the other.

Above right: On 14 August 1921, *Greenbrier* rammed and sank the Formby Channel Lightship *Planet*. Surprisingly, a photographer was on hand to record the tragic event. It was to be the last victim of *Moewe/Greenbrier*, which was itself sunk in Norway on 7 April 1945 after being bombed in Vadheimfjord.

Right: Greenbrier was transferred to the German company Midgard and renamed *Oldenburg* in 1933. Her sister, *Miami* (II), was completed in 1915 as *Pionier* for the Cameroons fruit service but never entered service during the war. She was used as a U-boat crew accommodation ship and handed to the British in 1919.

Left: The captain, officers and engineers of *Patuca* (I) at Avonmouth in 1921.

Right: A similar view of the deck officers and engineers of *Motagua* at Avonmouth in the same year.

Above left: From 1919 onwards, nineteen standardised ships were built for the line, with the last, *Corrales* entering service in 1930. The first ship to be launched was *Chirripo* (II), from Workman, Clark on 11 December 1919. The concept was that a weekly service could be operated to many European ports, consolidating Elders & Fyffes' near monopoly in the banana trade. The class was of approximately 5,400 grt and could carry 100,000 stems of bananas in their refrigerated holds. This view shows *Chirripo* on her maiden voyage.

Above right: *Chirripo* unloading to the wharf at Bremerhaven in 1925.

Right: *Chirripo* at Bremen, unloading bananas into coasters on the same voyage.

Left: *Zent* (II) was launched at Cammell Laird on 21 April 1920. The Cammell Laird ships could be distinguished by their slightly shorter funnels.

Right: *Reventazon* (II) was delivered from Workman, Clark in 1921. She had an uneventful career, being sold in 1935 to the German company Union Handels, becoming their *Bremerhaven*. She became a hospital ship and was sunk near Danzig on 31 October 1944.

Left: Manistee (II), another of the Cammell Laird vessels, was launched in October 1920 and entered service in January 1921. Powered by triple expansion engines, she had a single screw propeller. *Manistee* is shown here on the Mersey in a photograph, which was probably taken by B. A. Fielden. She became HMS *Manistee* during the Second World War and was sunk on 21 February 1941 in a combined attack by *U-107* and the Italian submarine *Bianchi*.

Right: Tortuguero (II), on a postcard issued in *c.* 1922.

Tortuguero lasted longer than most in her class, not being scrapped until 1958, when she was broken in Belgium.

Left: Bayano opened the Avonmouth Docks Extension in 1928.

Right: Bayano in the Royal Edward Dock, Avonmouth.

Above left: *Barranca* at Old Trafford, *c.* 1925.

Above right: *Pacuare* traversing the Manchester Ship Canal at Barton Bridge.

Left: *Pacuare* discharging her cargo at Avonmouth in the 1920s.

Left: Patia (II) in the Mersey, *c.* 1925. *Patia* was delivered from Cammell Laird in 1922 and sunk in April 1941, while operating as a catapult-armed merchantman, sporting a Hurricane fighter on a catapult on her bow.

Right: Aracataca (II) brand new out of Cammell Laird in 1924. So new, even, that B. A. Fielden has mis-spelled her name.

Left: Aracataca and *Tilapa* at Garston in December 1934. *Aracataca* was sunk near Rockall on a journey from Port Antonio, Jamaica, en route to Avonmouth on 30 November 1940. Thirty-six people lost their lives.

Below: Casanare, another of the Birkenhead-built ships, off Wallasey, *c.* 1930. Nine died when she was torpedoed by Otto Kretschmer's *U-99* on 3 November 1940. Shaw Savill's *Laurentic* stopped to pick up survivors and was herself sunk, followed by the *Patroculus*, of Blue Funnel Line.

Left: Cristales (1926) entering the dock system at Liverpool in the early 1930s. She too became a war casualty, being sunk on 12 May 1942 by British warships escorting Convoy ONS 92 after being crippled by the German submarine *U-124*'s torpedo attacks.

Right: Tetela outward bound on the Mersey, *c.* 1930.

Left: Tetela inward-bound on the Mersey. A postcard issued by Nautical Photo Agency.

Right: Tetela survived the war and was broken for scrap in Belgium in 1959.

S.S. "SULACO"

Left: The first *Sulaco* on the Mersey *c.* 1926, on a postcard by B. A. Fielden. She met her end at the hands of *U-124* south of Iceland on 20 October 1940. Sixty-three crew and two gunners were lost when she went down.

Right: *Tucarinca* and *Chagres* (II) were both built by Alexander Stephen on the Clyde, the former in 1926, the latter a year later.

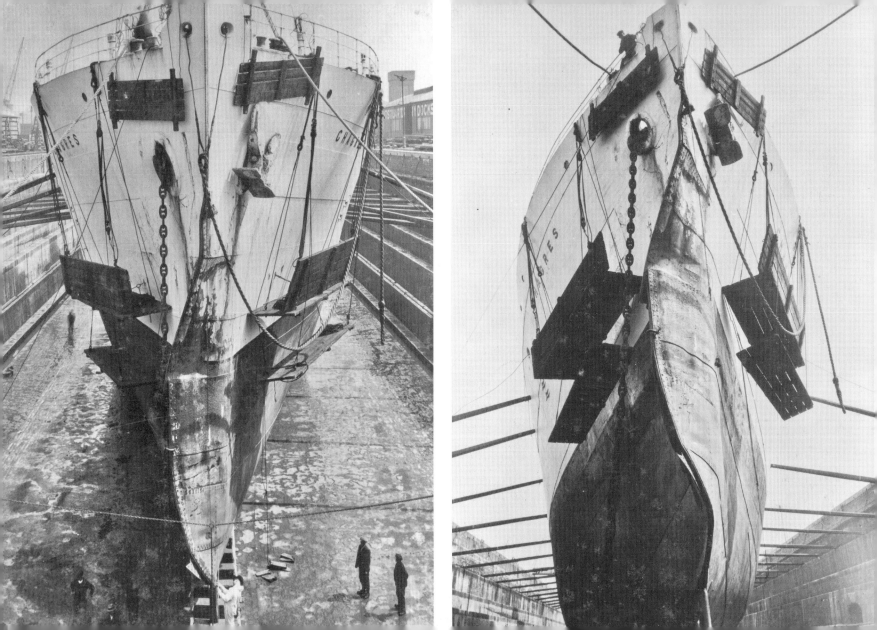

Right: Tilapa passing Carrington power station, Irlam, on the Manchester Ship Canal. She was completed in 1928 and, in 1945, brought the first bananas back to Britain after the war, importing ten million through Avonmouth that month. The power station has now been demolished and its site used to store brand new cars.

Right: Tilapa was scrapped in 1959 at Preston. Here she is in better times.

Opposite: Chagres collided with the *C.B. Pedersen*, a Norwegian sailing vessel, off the Azores in 1937. Here she is in dry dock in Avonmouth, sporting the damage caused when she sank the sailing vessel. *Chagres* rescued the crew of the *Pedersen*. She was sunk herself on 9 February 1940 after setting off a magnetic mine near the Bar lightship.

Nicoya (II) was built on the Clyde, at Alexander Stephen's yard, in 1929. She was the second ship to bear the name.

Samala off Rock Ferry. Built in Birkenhead, she was lost in 1940 when travelling alone from Kingston to Garston. Sunk by *U-62*, sixty-seven people died when she was sunk by gunfire.

Left: Nicoya (II) replaced her older sister, which was scrapped the year previously in Holland. This view shows her leaving Rotterdam for Dordrecht, where she was cut up.

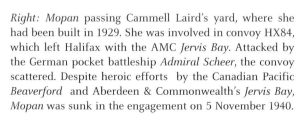

Right: Mopan passing Cammell Laird's yard, where she had been built in 1929. She was involved in convoy HX84, which left Halifax with the AMC *Jervis Bay*. Attacked by the German pocket battleship *Admiral Scheer*, the convoy scattered. Despite heroic efforts by the Canadian Pacific *Beaverford* and Aberdeen & Commonwealth's *Jervis Bay*, *Mopan* was sunk in the engagement on 5 November 1940.

Matina was deliverd in 1929, the penultimate of the nineteen vessels of the class. She disappeared during the Second World War and it is assumed that she was sunk by a combination of the U-boats *U-28* and *U-31* off Rockall in late October 1940.

Ten years after *Chirripo* came from Workman, Clark, *Corrales* was completed at Linthouse. She served during the war as a NAAFI store ship. She was the last of the nineteen standard ships. Here she is in the Mersey.

Corrales at Avonmouth, *c*. 1935.

Corrales sailing out of the Mersey with the Liver Building at her stern.

Mariposa (I) on the slip at Jamaica. This sailing tender was made of oak and was scrapped in 1928.

Above: Manistee making the first voyage into Rotterdam on I July 1923.

Right: Pacuare (I) docked, *c.* 1925.

Left: Cavina (II) on her sea trials on the Clyde. Built in 1924, she was the first of three new 'A' class liners. Carrying sixty First Class passengers, they offered round-trip cruises to Jamaica with three nights ashore for £45. She was 6,907 grt and 425 ft long.

Right: An aerial view of Cavina.

Left: Carare was completed at Cammell Laird in 1925. On 28 May 1940, she was sunk off Lynmouth, in the Bristol Channel, after hitting a mine and went down by the head. She is shown here at Avonmouth, with the banana conveyers behind her.

'The *Carare* on a permanent wave.

Right: A postcard issued for sale aboard *Carare* while she was cruising to Jamaica.

Ariguani loading in the West Indies. She was constructed in 1926 and her home port was Avonmouth.

Above left: The last of the three new 'A' ships, *Ariguani* was converted to a catapult armed merchantman during the war and had her stern blown off, as will be seen in the next chapter.

Above right: *Argual* on the Clyde, by W. Robertson.

Below left and right: *Telde, Argual* and *Orotava* were constructed for the Canary Islands trade, importing Cavendish bananas as well as tomatoes. They did not have refrigeration equipment but were fitted with forced air ventilation systems. The ships were smaller (2,500 grt) and of 314 ft length. All three were transferred to the Mayan SS Co. in 1933. *Telde* is shown here on her sea trials (left) and docked (right).

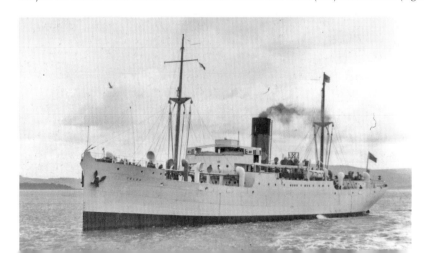

Above left: Orotava berthed in Bristol.

Above right: After transfer from Mayan SS Co., the ships went to Empresa Hondurena de Vapores in 1934 and after the war continued in service with United Fruit Co.

Left: Aztec, Toltec and *Mazatec* were the next three ships to enter service, acquired from United Fruit after the merger with their original owners, Cuyamel Fruit Co., Honduras, in 1930. A year later, the ships were transferred to Elders & Fyffes for the Honduras–Bremerhaven and Rotterdam routes. All three ships, of 5,502 grt, were built by Barclay, Curle of Glasgow. This views shows *Aztec* as *Peter Lassen*, as she became in 1938, when she was sold to Denmark. She was sold for scrap in 1961 and broken in Japan.

A stern view of *Toltec*. In 1938, she was renamed *Knud Rasmussen* and was scrapped in 1961 in Belgium.

Mazatec on her sea trials in her original Cuyamel Fruit Co. livery. She was scrapped in 1961 in Belgium.

Chapter Five

YES, WE HAVE NO BANANAS – WAR AGAIN

Yes, We Have no Bananas is the title of a song from the 1922 musical *Make it Snappy*. The phrase was made popular again during the Second World War, when bananas were not exported to Britain.

The war was to have a huge effect on Fyffes. Twenty-one vessels entered the war but only seven remained at its end. With the annexation of Kamerun, Elders & Fyffes ships began operating from Africa, bringing the first bananas to Britain in November 1939. The local banana plantations were also taken over by Elders & Fyffes but a decision made in 1940 was to have huge repercussions for the company. With so many losses to U-boats, the British wartime coalition government decided to restrict imports of fruits to one crop only. That chosen was oranges and, despite their popularity, bananas lost out. From November 1940 until December 1945, not a banana was to be seen in the United Kingdom. The company's plantations suffered too and all of the ships not converted to Navy uses were operated by the Ministry of Food and the Shipping Controller to bring much-needed foodstuffs to the UK. *Ariguani* had a chequered war career, having had her stern blown off, been converted to launch off aircraft and was also used as a troopship.

At the end of the war, Elders & Fyffes set about building up their plantations again, while awaiting the return of their vessels from war duties. In December 1945, no longer was the phrase 'yes, we have no bananas' heard. *Tilapa* imported ten million bananas just in time for Christmas. No doubt many banana splits were had that year. The banana split was invented in Latrobe, Pennsylvania, by David Evans Strickler, in 1904. That delicious pudding, created around a soda fountain in a Pennsylvania chemist's, is still a perennial favourite the world over, but must have been even more so after five banana-less years.

Twelve ships were managed for the Ministry of War Transport during the war and they included; *Brita Thorden*, *Empire Abbey*, *Empire Balfour*, *Empire Lady*, *Ester Thorden*, *Rosenburg*, *Samstrule* and *Yildum*.

Left: Wartime saw numerous losses, as well as some novel new uses for the Elders & Fyffes ships. *Ariguani* became a catapult-armed merchantman and led a colourful career through the war. The next series of images show her various uses and calamities that overcame her. Despite all of this, she managed to survive the war. *Ariguani* on an official painting for the line by Leonard Cusden.

Right: In August 1941, *Ariguani* was converted to carry a Fairey Fulmar supplied by 804 Squadron, Wick. The plan was that the fighter would engage with the long-range Focke Wulf Condor bombers that tailed convoys and the pilot would either make for land or ditch in the sea close to a rescue ship. She sailed for Sierra Leone in convoy and launched her first attack on 27 August 1941, about 300 miles from Bantry Bay, Cork, scaring off a Condor. The pilot landed in the Republic of Ireland and only the kindness of a local, who supplied gallons of petrol, saw the pilot escape to the North from internment in the South, where he promptly landed on a freshly-laid concrete runway, ruining it.

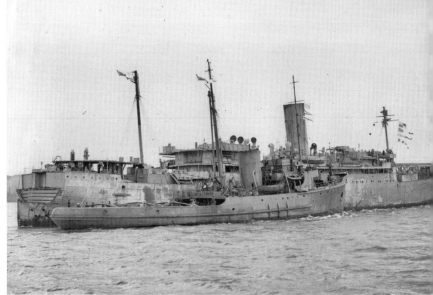

Above: Reaching the Clyde in February 1942, her stern patched with wood and concrete, *Ariguani* is escorted in by HMS *Samsonia*.

Left: On 26 October 1941, inbound from Gibraltar, *Ariguani* was torpedoed 400 miles west of Cape St Vincent, Portugal. Her stern was extensively damaged. She was abandoned but subsequently reboarded and recovered back to Gibraltar. She sailed for the Clyde after temporary repairs. Her Hurricane, as she was now fitted with (see previous page), had been launched and its commander, Birrell (who had ruined that runway in Northern Ireland) ditched and was rescued by HMS *Campion*.

Left: Once inside the safety of the Clyde, Steel & Bennie's tugs took over and hauled *Ariguani* to a shipyard for repair.

Right: Ariguani survived the war, as can be seen here in Hamilton, Bermuda in 1946. She was still in war service, and still has her anti-mine equipment on her bow, as well as quick-launch lifeboats on her sides.

Chapter Six

TALLY ME BANANA – THE POST-WAR YEARS

'Tally me Banana' comes from the *Banana Boat Song*, made famous by Harry Belafonte in 1956, but a Jamaican folk song inspired by the loading of bananas on the night shift, with the workers awaiting the Tally Man to count the stems they have loaded and pay them accordingly.

Seven ships survived the war, fourteen were lost, so fierce was the U-boat war in the Atlantic. Few people realise just how dangerous the Battle of the Atlantic was but its story is one of human lives lost and ships that had taken a year of building, but that had gone down in a matter of minutes. As war reparation, Elders & Fyffes again acquired ships from the German firm Laeisz. This time, four vessels came into the fleet, and they operated the Cameroons route they had been built for. Only the destination had changed – Britain, instead of Germany. Ships were chartered to make up the shortfall of vessels and, in 1949, the banana plantations of Dominica started producing in quantity. A year later, the company's largest vessel yet entered service. The passenger vessel *Golfito* was a radical departure for Fyffes, and was too large to call into some of the smaller ports and harbours the company's ships visited.

Between 1953 and 1956 the company gained from the government restrictions on dollar-based imports and banana imports doubled to 263,500 tons, but lost out on tariff charges in the Canary Islands, and their trade from there effectively collapsed. In 1958, United Fruit decided to cut back on its fleet and Fyffes inherited three of their vessels. Much thought was now made as to how the companies would operate their fleets. Surrey Shipping Co. was formed to own ships, but the vessels would be managed by Elders & Fyffes. The Surrey Shipping vessels were primarily used on the US routes. The period also saw many of the older Fyffes vessels go to the scrapyard. Some coal-burners had gone as being uneconomical but some more recent tonnage went the same way too as Fyffes grappled with the problem of how to operate their fleet.

The independence of the Cameroons in 1962 also saw the effective loss of the plantations, which were nationalised, and new laws decreed that 50 per cent of the banana boats had to be Cameroons-registered. By 1964, the Cameroon trade was over. The year previous, Elders & Fyffes had begun to diversify out of bananas by purchasing George Munro Ltd, a fruit and vegetable distributor. In April 1964, George Jackson & Co. was purchased, and a string of smaller acquisitions followed. A rationalisation of home ports took place too and Garston closed in July 1965, with Avonmouth closing in February 1967, ending a link with the port that dated back to 1901.

In 1968, McCann's, which had now become Torney Brothers & McCann Ltd, amalgamated with United Fruit Importers and Connolly Shaw to become Fruit Importers of Ireland Ltd. This organisation would ultimately own Elders & Fyffes, which changed its name to Fyffes Group Ltd in 1969. This name change coincided with a transfer of ships away from United Fruit to Fyffes, with seven vessels changing owner. In 1970, Fyffes' boats were repainted with the United Fruit livery. United Fruit itself had become United Brands Corporation. Passenger-carrying ceased in 1972, with the loss of the *Golfito* and *Camito*. The 1973 Arab-Israeli war saw fuel prices leap and Fyffes' most uneconomic ships went. The rest of the seventies was a period of transition as ships were chartered rather than owned, where possible.

In 1981, United Brands concentrated all its ship-owning on Fyffes Line Ltd and Elders & Fyffes as a name disappeared forever. Only *Almirante* was left by 1984, all other vessels having been sold. Fyffes was put up for sale in 1986 and Fruit Importers of Ireland purchased the brand for £26.5m. Most importantly, the major competition, Geest, was purchased in 1996. The company today still goes from strength to strength, its Fyffes brand instantly recognizable to millions in Britain and overseas. The company employs many thousands in the Caribbean, and has been well known over the years as a major benefactor and improver of lives for its workers. Long may it continue.

Of course, the time comes now for yet more banana facts! Bananas are a great source of potassium and fibre. They are also related to manila hemp and the bird of paradise flower. It is also considered that the banana and its close relative, the plantain, originated in Asia but have become staple crops the world over. The banana is nature's perfect package, a healthy, nutritious snack contained within a thick skin that protects the fruit from dirt and dust as much as it does from mucky fingers.

Pacuare (II) was a war prize. Built at the Bremer, Vulkan yard in Vegesack in 1934, she was originally the *Pelikan* for Laeisz's Cameroons banana service and was acquired by Elders & Fyffes in 1946. *Pacuare* at Liverpool on 27 June 1954.

Pacuare at Garston, *c.* 1950.

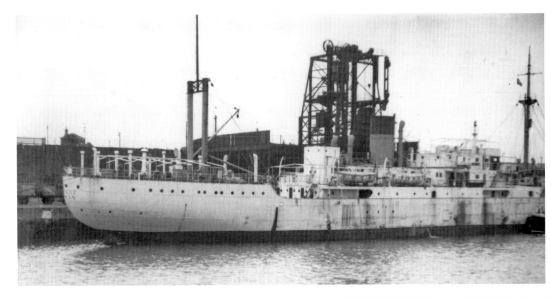

Left and below: Pacuare leaves Garston on 21 September 1959 to be broken at Troon, Scotland. She is photographed from *Nicoya* (III).

Right and below: Nicoya (III) was also built for the Cameroons service in 1935 as *Pontos* (below). She entered Fyffes service in 1947 after a spell as *Mowddach,* for the Ministry of War Transport. This view (right) shows her in the Mersey.

Above left: Nicoya leaving Garston to go to the breaker's yard on 21 September 1959.

Above right: Beached in the ships' graveyard, Briton Ferry, ready to be scrapped in late September 1959.

Below: Reventazon (III) was the third vessel acquired by Elders & Fyffes from the MOWT. Her original name was *Panther* and she saw war service in Norway as well as a U-boat submarine target ship. For this, she was renamed *Salzburg* as the Kreigsmarine already had another *Panther*. She is shown here at Garston.

At Southampton's berth 101, photographed from Mayflower Park, *Reventazon* discharges her cargo of bananas in 1962.

Reventazon at the Fyffes banana terminal at Southampton docks on 9 June 1961. She was sold in 1963 and eventually scrapped in the winter of 1973 at Kaohsiung, China.

Right: Zent (III) was also a war prize, being built in Denmark in 1938 and fitted with Burmeister & Wain diesel engines. At Garston, on 22 December 1957.

Below left and right: Zent in tow for Brugge, where she was scrapped in July 1962.

Left: Manistee (III) was built at Workman, Clark in 1932 for the Erin Steam Ship Co. and originally named *Eros.* She entered Fyffes service in 1946 and had the first cruiser stern on a company ship. Shown here in London's West India Dock on 4 October 1949.

Right: Manistee was rebuilt in 1958, as shown here on the Mersey.

Left: At John Cashmore's Newport, Monmouthshire, shipbreaking yard on 25 May 1960.

Right: Matina (III), the first turbine steamer for Elders & Fyffes. Is shown here off Dover outward bound from Rotterdam back to the Caribbean. She was capable of carrying 221,000 stems of bananas in her holds.

Above: Matina at Southampton, 1962. In 1967, Southampton became the main terminal in the UK for importation of Fyffes bananas, after the closure of Avonmouth.

Left: Matina sporting some bow damage after collision, with *Stanwear* and *Algol* in the background.

Above: Matina at Southampton, 24 August 1968.

Rightt: In 1949 came the company's biggest ship to date, the 8,736 grt *Golfito*. She was a radical departure from the normal Fyffes ships and could accommodate ninety-nine passengers and had a crew of seventy-four. Built at the Stephen's yard at Linthouse, she had twin turbines and a maximum speed of 19 kt, which she easily achieved on her sea trials off Arran.

Golfito sailed from Avonmouth to Trinidad, Barbados and Jamaica on a monthly service and is shown here at Barbados.

Golfito's home port soon changed to Southampton, when she also offered a service to Rotterdam.

Above: At Southampton on 20 April 1950, where her home berth was in the Empress Dock.

Right: Golfito in Southampton, 1962. She had been overhauled in 1956 and a swimming pool included.

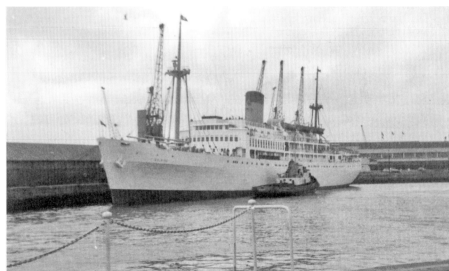

Left: Golfito outward-bound from Southampton on 26 July 1960.

Right: This gorgeous little ship finally met her end in 1972, after reaching Shipbreaking Industries' shipbreaking yard at Faslane on 31 December 1971. She followed in the footsteps of such ships as Cunard's *Aquitania*, which was also broken at Faslane.

Golfito was powered by twin turbines and had two screws. She had 10,000 shp at 125 rpm.

Left: Golfito at Southampton, 21 May 1966.

Below: March 1952 and three of Fyffes' ships are berthed at Avonmouth.

S.S. CAVINA   FRIDAY 19.10.51

FAREWELL DINNER

Tomato Cocktail   Grapefruit Oporto

Hors d'oeuvres

Stuffed Olives   Queen Olives
Anchovy Fillets   Silver Skin Onions
Smoked Salmon   Salami Sausage

Consomme Macedoine   Potage American

Boiled Salmon – Hollandaise Sauce
Fillet of Halibut – Maitre d'Hotel

Asparagus Vinaigrette
Fillet Mignons – Bordelaise

Baked Cumberland Ham – Sweet Corn
Garden Peas   Steamed Rice
Browned & Boiled Potatoes
Roast Norfolk Turkey – St Hubert

COLD : Roast Pork   Roast Beef
Ox Tongue   Oxford Brawn
Roast Lamb   Galantine of Chicken

Salad : Sliced Beetroot
Vinaigrette Dressing

Plum Pudding – Brandy Sauce
Strawberry Chantilly
Assorted Marzipan Fruits
Ice Cream & Wafers

Dessert   Coffee

Above and left: A Farewell Dinner menu for *Cavina* from 19 October 1951. Rather surprisingly, despite the abundance of them in the hold, no bananas are on the menu.

Above: Cavina in the Royal Edward Dock, Avonmouth, in July 1953. In 1946, *Cavina* was chartered to Cunard as the banana plantations in Jamaica had been neglected throughout the war and would take time to be readied for post-war farming.

Below: Cavina in the Royal Edward Dock, July 1953.

Above left and right: Cavina was sold out of service in 1957 to the Barkstone Shipping Co., of Hong Kong, and scrapped there in 1958. She was renamed *Barkstone* for the rest of her career. These two views show her final departure from Avonmouth. The tug *Bristolian* pulls her away from the wharf for the last time.

Right: Ariguani berthed in the Royal Edward Dock, Avonmouth, next to the turning basin, September 1953. Her Blue Peter is flying, signifying that she is ready to leave on another voyage to the West Indies.

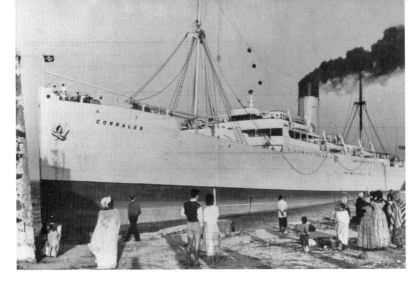

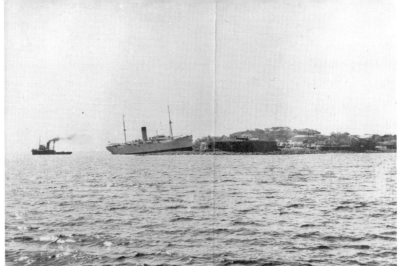

Above left and right: *Corrales* was to suffer her own rather embarrassing incident in 1958 at Goree Island, Dakar, Senegal, when she ran aground. These two views show her aground, while onlookers stand amazed at the ship on the shore.

Left: The Greek steamer *Rita*, heavily listing, after her cargo of timber has shifted. She is berthed next to *Corrales*, which was registered in Glasgow.

Above left: Laid up at Garston, *Corrales* is prepared for her final voyage to the breaker's yard.

Above right: Towed out of the Mersey on 17 May 1961, *Corrales* makes her final voyage. She was broken at Santander, Spain.

Right: Bayano (II) at Kingston, Jamaica, on her final voyage back to the UK. She reached Avonmouth on 28 December 1955, having made 280 transatlantic journeys and having carried over 3,000 million bananas to Europe.

Above left: After her record-breaking voyages, *Sea Queen* pulls *Bayano* away from the quayside on 3 January 1956 en route to Ghent to be broken up by Van Heyghen Frères.

Above right: The launch of *Camito* in March 1956 from Alexander Stephen's yard on the Clyde. She included a cinema and a swimming pool as part of her design. Fyffes had already noticed the drop in passenger traffic due to the advent of jet aircraft. She was the last large passenger ship built for Elders & Fyffes.

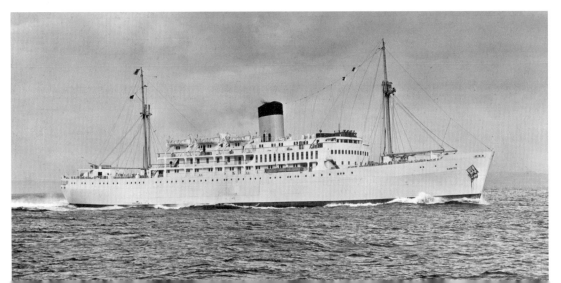

Left: Camito on her sea trials. A mere sixteen years after her maiden voyage from Greenock on 12 November 1956, she sailed for Japan. Leaving there on 31 March 1973, she sailed for Kaohsiung, and the slow process of being cut up for scrap.

Camito surrounded by tugs as she leaves port.

Camito at Southampton on 20 September 1967.

Left: Camito replaced *Ariguani,* which was now surplus to requirements. Leaving Avonmouth for the final time, on a dark winter's night, ghostly figures watch the departure on the dockside.

Right: Ariguani is cast off and begins her short journey to Briton Ferry, where she will be cut up.

At her final berth, the only bananas *Ariguani* is likely to see now are the ones brought into the yard in packed lunches, as snacks for the men who will cut her up over the next few months.

Right and below right: Mariposa (II) on her trials on the Thames. The first image shows her at Chelsea Reach. She was of fibreglass construction and was 31 ft long and 10 ft wide.

Above: A sailing list from 1968, with *Camito* or *Golfito* on its cover.

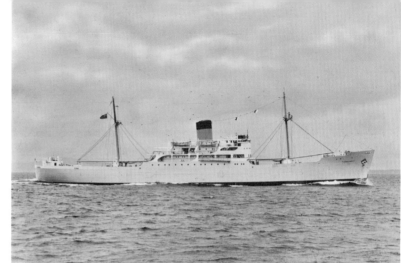

Above left: Between 1957 and 1961, Stephen's built four smaller ships, still of 6,300-6,400 grt, for the Cameroon banana trade that Fyffes had built up. The first was *Changuinola* (II), which was delivered in September 1957 and she is shown here arriving at Liverpool for her maiden arrival.

Above right: *Changuinola* on her sea trials. She travelled back up the Clyde to Dalmuir on 6 April 1975 be broken at the long-established yard of W. H. Arnott Young & Co.

Right: *Chirripo* (III) entering the enlarged dry dock at Birkenhead on 6 October 1960.

Chirripo out of her natural element for what was probably her first dry-docking. In 1974, she was broken up.

Above: Chicanoa on her sea trials in 1958.

Above: Chuscal was last of the quartet and entered service in 1961. She was scrapped in 1974 at Inverkeithing after a mere thirteen years of service. She is shown here off Arran on her sea trials in February 1961.

Right: Chicanoa getting a badly needed repaint at some point in the mid-1960s. Between 1970 and 1972, after the Cameroons trade had died away, all four ships were sold. *Chicanoa* was broken up in Dalmuir in 1974.

Above: Chuscal at Newhaven, Sussex in 1970, the year the ships' colour schemes changed from silver grey hull, with buff funnel and black top, to white hull, with the United Fruit red with white diamond funnel.

Below: Manistee outward bound from the Mersey, passing *Tortuguero* on her final voyage in October 1958.

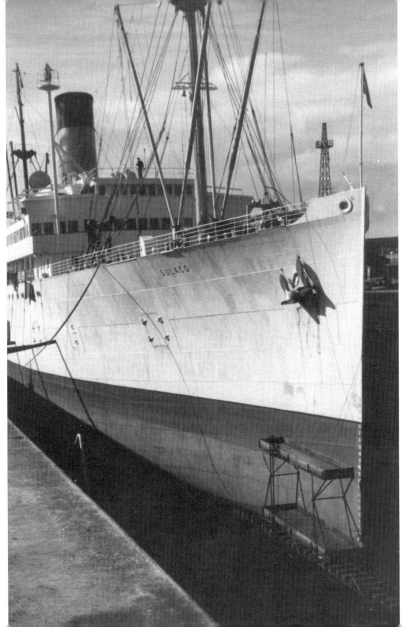

Above and right: *Sulaco* loading in the West Indies.

Opposite right Despite being built in 1931, *Sulaco* (II) only entered Fyffes'
service in 1958, with her maiden voyage for Fyffes being from Hampton Roads
to Jamaica and then Avonmouth. She is seen here in dry dock in Southampton
in 1962.

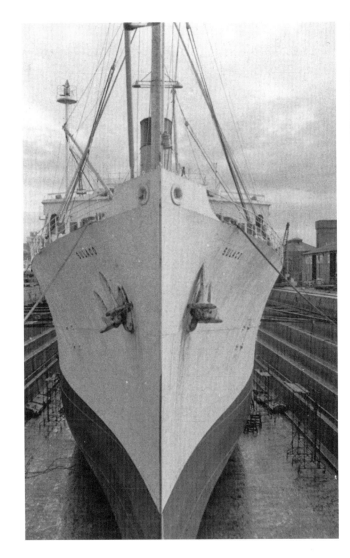

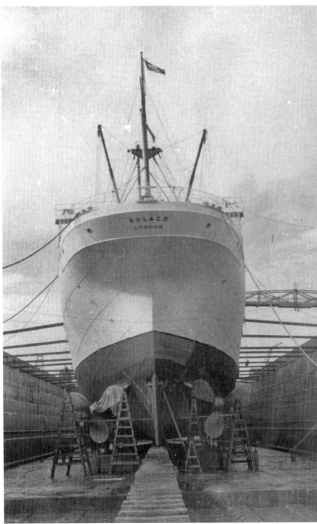

Sulaco in the Mount Stuart dry dock at Cardiff.

Right and below right: Samala (II) was constructed in 1932 as *Quirigua* for United Fruit and entered service for Elders & Fyffes in January 1959. She had a short career with Fyffes before being sold for scrap in 1962. She was broken up at Kaohsiung. Shown here in the Empress Dock, Southampton, just before her final voyage to the breaker's yard.

Below: Sulaco was only intended to be in service for five years and was scrapped in Bruges in 1964.

Sinaloa being towed into Bruges by the tug *Rolf Gerling* to be broken. Her sister, *Sulaco*, is already cut down to her main deck.

Turrialba, built in 1960 at Bremer, Vulkan, was the first of six ships built for Surrey Shipping Co., but managed by Fyffes. She was 451 ft long, had four decks of holds and could carry a quarter of a million stems of bananas. She is shown here at Vegesack, Germany, before her maiden voyage. She ended her sailing career on 27 February 1980 at Kaohsiung after running aground the previous September in the Philippines.

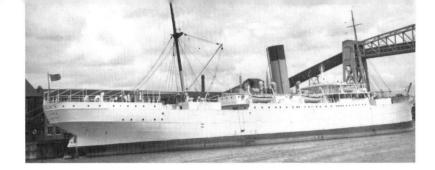

Right above, middle and below: Tilapa (I) at Ward's yard at Preston for breaking. Thos W. Ward, based in Sheffield had numerous shipbreaking yards around the UK, from Briton Ferry, Neath, South Wales, to Inverkeithing and Rosyth in Scotland. They broke many famous ships from White Star's first *Majestic*, in their Morecambe yard to Cunard's Blue Riband holder *Mauretania* (I) in their Rosyth base and *Mauretania* (II) and *Ark Royal* at Inverkeithing.

Above: Turrialba at Wilmington West basin, Los Angeles, on 25 July 1970. Although registered in London, the ship spent most of her career sailing between the Caribbean and New York.

Below: Tenadores at Wilmington West basin, Los Angeles, 1960. Twenty years later, she was scrapped by Kang Hua Enterprise Co., which had contracted to buy all six of the fleet as they completed their last voyages in late 1979/80.

Above: Tenadores was second of the sextet. Surrey Shipping Co., her owner, was a subsidiary of United Fruit Co. This view shows her on her maiden voyage at New Orleans.

Above left and right: Bow damage to *Tetela* at the Todd Shipyards, Brooklyn, NY. The later photo shows her on 21 July 1965.

Tetela (II) at Wilmington West basin, Los Angeles, on 11 July 1960.

Telde (II) arrived in 1961, In 1974 she was laid up in Barry Docks, then transferred to Empresa Hondurena de Vapores SA. She arrived at Kaohsiung on 25 December 1979, the first to be scrapped.

Tucurinca (II), built in 1962.

Above left and right: *Matina* (IV) was built at Kobe, Japan, and was the fourth Fyffes ship to bear the name and the first of a fleet of eight new vessels designed to be able to carry all sorts of chilled produce from oranges to fresh meat, and bananas to frozen fish. These two views show her launch from the Kawasaki Heavy Industries shipyard.

Morant entered service in January 1970. She is shown here in London, at berth 25, West India dock, on 27 June 1970. She sailed from there to Canada on Thursday 2 July 1970. Her name brought back associations with *Port Morant*, the Imperial Direct steamer of Elder Dempster. The other ships of the set were *Motagua* (II), *Manistee* (IV), *Mazatec* (II), *Magdalena* and *Manzanares* (II).

The Fyffes fleet, 1987, showing ships past and present. Those more modern vessels, either managed or owned by the company until this date include:

Darien, built 1964, entering Fyffes service in 1974 and managed by Salen UK Ship Management.

Davao, her sister, also acquired in 1974. In 1981, she became *Chion Trader* and was scrapped in January 1985.

Barranca, designed for the Puerto Cortes-Galveston route for United Fruit but transferred to Fyffes for the service in 1972. Laid up 1984 and sold for scrap 1985.

Bayano (III), built 1972, scrapped at Brownsville, Texas, 1985.

Almirante, built 1970 as a fish carrier, used as a fruit carrier mid-1970s.

Jarikaba and *Nickerie*, both chartered to Fyffes in 1986 on the Surinam–UK route.

Coppename and *Cottica*, built in Japan in 1990 and 1991 for charter to Fyffes.

Musa in the English Channel. She was sold in 1982 to Arabian owners and renamed *Al Zahrah*.